THREE JUDGES

YAHWEH'S VICTORIES:

STORM'S FURY, DECEITFUL STRATAGEMS, AND LUSTFUL DESIRE

REV. STEPHEN CROWELL, MDIV.

L.E. CAPODAGLI

INTRODUCTION BY

L.E. CAPODAGLI

Three Judges

Yahweh's Victories: Storm's Fury, Deceitful Stratagems, and Lustful Desire

Rev. Stephen Crowell, Mdiv

© 2011 by Wave Dancer Productions
Rushford, New York

All rights reserved. No portion of this book may be used in any form without the written permission the publishers, with the exception of brief excerpts in magazine articles, reviews, etc.

Printed in the United States

Produced by Wave Dancer Productions
Post Office Box 64
Rushford, NY 14777

If you have any questions or comments concerning this book please contact the Rev. Crowell at pastor@konxions.org.

New Revised Standard Version Bible, copyright © 1989 National Council of the Churches of Christ in the United States of America. Used by permission. All rights reserved.

"Revised Standard Version of the Bible, copyright 1952 [2nd edition, 1971] by the Division of Christian Education of the National Council of the Churches of Christ in the United States of America. Used by permission. All rights reserved."

Scripture quotations marked (NIV) are taken from the Holy Bible, New International Version®, NIV®. Copyright © 1973, 1978, 1984, 2011 by Biblica, Inc.™ Used by permission of Zondervan. All rights reserved worldwide. www.zondervan.com.

Scripture quotations are taken from the Holy Bible, New Living Translation, copyright ©1996, 2004, 2007 by Tyndale House Foundation. Used by permission of Tyndale House Publishers, Inc., Carol Stream, Illinois 60188. All rights reserved.

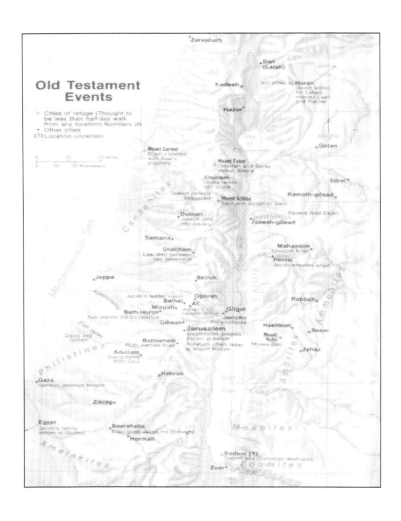

Biblestudy.org

TABLE OF CONTENTS

Acknowledgements	6
Introduction by L.E. Capodagli	8

Yahweh's intervention through a "Storm's Fury"

Deborah: Prophetess, Judge Warrior	20

Yahweh's intervention through "Deceitful Stratagems"

Gideon: From Winnowing to Testing To Victory	46

Yahweh's intervention through "Lustful Desires"

Sampson: The Judge who throws temper tantrums	74

About the Authors

Stephen Crowell	109
L. E. Capodagli	111

Acknowledgments

Three Judges steps into a different path than what we have done in the past sermon series. We took up the challenge to dig deep into the historical perspective of some of the "whys" the people of Israel would be tempted to move away from a God that had protected them so many times over the course of their history. The time involved in this particular project dug a little deeper into those family and recreational times. I (Stephen) wish to express my gratitude to Kristan and the kids for their patience. Just remember vacation is coming and I will leave the research home this time.

Hey there! First of all, I (Lee) would like to thank Stephen for giving me the opportunity to join forces with him in these various writing projects. It has been a very cool experience. I also want to throw out a big "Thank you" to Pastor Jonathan Finley (Rushford Baptist Church) for advice on the finer details of ancient Israeli religious life that helped me flesh out the narrative character who begins the Introduction.

THREE JUDGES:

A BRIEF LOOK AT

DEBORAH, GIDEON AND SAMPSON

Imagine that you are standing at the top of a long, steep, sandy slope strewn with rocks. The land drops steadily away before you in rough, irregular ridges. Behind you lies an endless stretch of hot, burning land. Here and there clumps of small boulders break through the monotony of the dunes. The rising sun burns hot upon your weather-beaten face. The air is still, not a breath of wind stirs, and you can feel the heat of the sand pushing up through the souls of your worn sandals. Your feet have stirred from the sand a small brown *gecoq*, a fearful little soul of a lizard common to your homeland, and he scurries across your toes to his next hiding place, piping out his two-note call of alarm. High above you in the cloudless sky, a Black Kite circles slowly on the faint morning breeze, his keen eyes searching for perhaps just such a breakfast morsel. Despite the coming heat of the new day the dawn is chilly, and you clutch your robe more tightly to yourself, those dreadful words still echoing hollowly in your mind: "Joshua is dead!" The cry had carried ghost-like down the streets of your village just as the pale rose streaks of dawn began to color the desert sky. You had risen in haste and rushed to the top of the knoll to hear the news yourself from the caravan that had traveled all night to bring the grave tidings.

You squint to shield your eyes from the glare of the rising sun and examine the land that lies before you, wondering for the thousandth time how you ever managed to end up here. At the bottom of the slope the land springs into a sudden rich greenness, a winding band that runs snake-like down the middle of the valley toward the well-tended lowlands laid out with back-breaking effort into neat rectangular plots radiating outward from the camp in a hub. You kick angrily at the sand.

"I shall bring you up out of the affliction of Egypt...unto a land flowing with milk and honey," you mutter to yourself. Un-huh. Sand and lizards and enemies were more like it. Thank goodness at least some of the natives had been willing to help you learn the finer tricks of bringing water and life to the drier regions of the desert. Too bad it was all so mixed up with their stinking little alien gods. Sometimes it was hard to reconcile all the things they told you that you had to do to have a good crop, and the things your priests kept saying. Still, it had been a good year....

A long wail drifts up the slope from the village. The women would be gathering in the village square now to weep and mourn, mourn and weep. Your mind wanders back to the last time you went to the meeting tent to hear the priests read from the scriptures: "In the sweat of your face you shall eat bread till you return to the ground, for out of it you were taken; you are dust, and to dust you shall return." For some reason the words had stuck in your mind then; you don't know why. You kick at the sand again. Joshua--Joshua dead! Why? Yes, he was a man of many years...but dead? Now what? What would happen *now*?

Enter the Judges of Israel.

*   *   *   *   *

To better understand the three judges that Stephen has chosen to focus on in this book it may help to remember what the situation was as we come into that period in the history of Israel.

The period of the Judges is generally viewed as occurring between circa 1380 B.C. (Joshua had died eight years earlier) and circa 1045 B.C. (the United Monarchy of Israel was founded in 1050 B.C.). As the book opens, Moses' God-appointed successor, Joshua, has just died. The Israelites occupy the land promised to them, but they do not control it. Due to their disobedience, remnants of all the partially conquered native people groups still live amongst them, free to sow a wide band of sinful seed the Israelites seem more than ready to harvest. A dwindling willingness for personal commitment to God, social and civil breakdown and the inability of the tribes to work in unison were the results of this mixing of peoples. Just as it does not take much extra salt to spoil the flavor of a whole pot of soup, so it did not take a large alien influence upon the Israelites to spoil their taste for the whole "pot of God".

Now, the three judges we will be looking at--as were all the judges--were caught in what Stephen terms the "spin cycle": a cycle of repetitive, self-destructive behaviors committed by the people of Israel.

The cycle begins with the Israelites following God faithfully under a strong leader. Then the leader dies and the people begin to fall away from the worship of the true God (apostasy) and begin to do things just because they seemed right to them: *"In those days Israel had no king; all the people did whatever seemed right in their own eyes."* (Judges 17:6; 18:1; 19:1; 21:25 RSV) Having deserted Yahweh, Yahweh leaves them in the hands of their oppressors. After a period of great oppression, Israel turns back to their God and cries out for His mercy. The Lord raises up yet another charismatic figure to lead them out of extremely difficult circumstances and restore their independence- -and their worship of Yahweh- -once again. This pattern is repeated a total of six times in the Book of Judges.

It is important to take a moment here to note briefly the biblical difference between a "judge" and a "king". The Hebrew title of the book is *Shophetim,* literally meaning "judges", although the character and actions of these individuals might more appropriately render the translation "saviors" or "deliverers". They were individuals to whom God had given the gift of leadership and raised up to act as popular heroes for the people. These individuals were charismatic (gifted) leaders, their power coming through divine appointment. They had no official standing.

Kings, on the other hand, represented "official" authority; power not given directly by God, but flowing from an office or appointment. They would typically be the administrators in the political and military sphere.

Due to this important distinction, we can now recognize that the "office" of judge was not a national appointment or election; not all the people were bound by edict to follow the same person. Judges generally had a limited and local following, in most cases probably just the villages that would have been within a proximity that allowed for reasonable travel and communication between each other. The number of people involved (population density) the distance between villages, and geographical features that limited movement (bodies of water, ranges of cliffs and mountains, lack of naturally occurring water) would all have led to naturally defined geological spheres of influence for the judges.

Note; however, that does not mean that the lines of jurisdiction were *strictly* defined. "On the spot" rule may have been--well, the general rule, not a law. It is entirely possible that in some scattered regions the allegiance of a village, or even of a family (consider it comparable to the divisions that occurred during the American Civil War), might be split between two roughly equidistant judges, depending simply upon personal preference.

Bear in mind also that nowhere in scripture is it even hinted at that we have been given a complete list or sequencing of all the Judges. This would easily provide an explanation for the fact that while some of the Judges are sequentially linked in scripture: *"After Ehud, Shamgar son of Anath rescued Israel."* (Judges 3:31 NLT) In other instances it is clear that at least two long-tenured judges were actively engaged in defending and ruling over specific and separate parts of Canaan.

"So the Lord burned with anger against Israel, and he turned them over to the Philistines and the Ammonites, who began to oppress them that year. For eighteen years they oppressed all the Israelites east of the Jordan River in the land of the Amorites (that is, in Gilead). The Ammonites also crossed to the west side of the Jordan and attacked Judah, Benjamin, and Ephraim." (Judges 10:7-9 NLT)

Areas of Influence for Israel's Judges

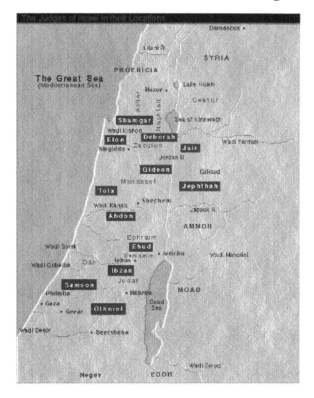

Consulting this map of Israel you can see that the land of Gilead was located basically north of the Dead Sea.

"Now Jephthah of Gilead was a great warrior...At about this time the Ammonites began their war against Israel. When the Ammonites attacked, the elders of Gilead sent for Jephthah in the land of Tob. The elders said, "Come and be our commander! Help us fight the Ammonites!" ...Jephthah said to the elders, "Let me get this straight. If I come with you and the Lord gives me victory over the

Ammonites, will you really make me ruler over all the people?" The Lord is our witness," the elders replied. "We promise to do whatever you say." (Judges 11:1; 4; 9; 10 NLT)

Clearly this was an "on the spot" appointment to fill a specific need of the people, and Jephthah was rewarded with a leadership (judge) position by the elders of Gilead. Sampson, on the other hand, was not only brought into a judgeship position by a different means (13:5 NLT), he was given a different area of Canaan to protect. Examine the map again. You will note that the Sampson controlled an area primarily west of the Dead Sea, probably 60-70 miles as the crow flies from the area where Jephthah battled the Ammonites.

Now let's take a moment and dig a little deeper at the root cause of the cyclic apostasy that started the Israelites on their cycle of sin time and time again. It was, of course, that ole pain-in-the-neck Baal. Look at it this way: one of the problems the Israelis had faced was a change of occupation and lifestyle. When the tribes came down out of the hills and settled into the new land they were not farmers, they were shepherds. It would have been only natural for them to seek out the farming wisdom of the people who had already learned how to tame and turn the dry desert land to agriculture.

Problem: many of the "tricks of the trade" of the Canaanite farmers involved worship of and allegiance to the local god Baal. These practices appealed to the sensual and materialistic yearnings of the Israelites who were used to an austere and almost antiseptic god. Dalliance with the prostitutes at the temple of Baal was a "guaranteed" cure-all in all matters regarding fertility (both vegetable and human). Other special rituals and sacrifices to Baal would further incur the favor of the god and could even bend his will to yours. Little wonder the neophyte Israeli farmers saw no difficulty in adapting to this new manner of securing divine blessings.

Next problem involving Baal: ironically, while Baal was the supreme Canaanite god, he was also represented as being the "little guy on the block". He was a "home town" god, known in each community by a distinct personal title. Baal was not the guy to go to if you wanted huge miraculous wonders, but hey, if you want better sugar beets in the lower forty, he's your guy. (Just go to the temple after dark with a little silver in hand--ask for Lola.) The Israelites had no problem serving Yahweh as a "national" god and Baal as the "local guy". So what was the Israelites problem? *Yahweh* had a problem with it, that's what. The old "if-it's-the-bosses-problem-it's-your-problem" syndrome, and yup, looks like it's time for another big helping of whoop-butt oppression by the feisty natives of Canaan.

Now, in this Introduction I have not attempted to make any effort to present a theory of authorship for Judges. Nor does Stephen, I believe, address this as an issue of great significance in his treatment of the subject matter. Regardless of who recorded the struggles of the judge's attempts to save a stubborn, mule-headed, at times infuriatingly blasphemous, at times-sweet-as-sugar people, the judges all faced multitudinous challenges in righting a ship that every new generation of Israelites seemed to have forgotten how to sail.

I have also not attempted to offer a thorough discussion of all the factors leading up to the events that our three judges under inspection become embroiled in. That would be an interesting study in itself, but it would not serve the purpose of this book. I believe in this case it is sufficient to simply put it as succinctly as comedic British author Douglas Adams did in his *Hitchhikers Guide To The Galaxy* trilogy. Adams was considering how you decide which people should be allowed to rule other people since the people who *want* to rule over other people are, probably, the ones least suited to do so. Adams' conclusion: "People are a problem." That was as true 3,500 years ago as it is today.

On the other hand, if you are a stickler for "religious stuff" (this *is* a "religious book") I could probably refer you to 2 Timothy 3:16-17: *"All scripture is inspired by God and profitable for teaching, for reproof, for correction, and for training in righteousness, that the man of God may be complete, equipped for every good work"*. (The Bible, hunh? I hear it's a pretty good reference work.) Get (or get out) a good study Bible and read Judges through in one sitting. It's fascinating stuff.

Finally, don't let Stephen's and my seeming irreverence for the subject matter lead you to believe we don't take this stuff seriously--we do. It's just that I happen to agree with Stephen when he says that sometimes you have to put a little bit of flesh and fat on the bones; liven up the dry old skeleton a bit. Did Gideon's father and

Sampson's mother really exist? Of course! (See that Bible thingy I mentioned.) Did they ever really set down the narratives as Stephen recounts them? Unh, well--excuse me, I think someone's at the door.

(Funny, nobody there; must have been the wind.) Anyway, as I was saying, while we have taken a little literary license with some of the material it is purely for the purpose of illustration, education, and yes, even entertainment. If it piques your interest and leads to a more in-depth exploration of scripture to find out what it *really* says—well, it's worth every minute and every made-up scenario.

So; go; read; I'm done rationalizing. A great selection of historical (and occasionally hysterical) figures awaits you. Enjoy.

"Deborah" - by Gustav Dore (French artist, 1832-1883)

Yahweh's intervention through a "Storm's Fury"

Deborah:

Prophetess, Judge, Warrior

Historical Setting

Our study of Deborah officially starts in the fourth chapter of Judges. It is here that we find that the Israelites have again fallen out of favor with God. Ehud had died and they again had forgotten who they served and did what was evil in the sight of the Lord. They were again facing the consequence of their sinful behavior. The Israelites turned their loyalty away from God to chase after the Canaanite god Baal.

The problems that Deborah faced began long before she was sitting under the palm trees judging the problems that came her way. It all started with Joshua and his failure to totally drive out or kill all of the different people groups that lived in the Promised Land. God, with complete wisdom about people full of weaknesses, had given them this commandment so that their lives would not be compromised. The pattern that the Israelites developed began with Joshua and continued to worsen under the first three judges (Othniel, Ehud, and Shamgar).

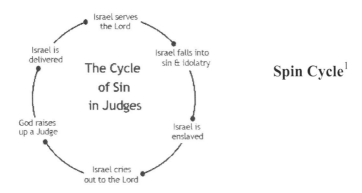

Spin Cycle[1]

The detrimental pattern or **Spin Cycle** begins with the Israelites faithfully worshiping God and following God's servant leader. Then, after the death of the servant leader, they begin to forget that they were children of God. Soon the Israelites begin to follow after the culture of the very people they were to eradicate. Their sons and daughters begin to intermarry with those who are still living in the land. It is then that their children begin to compromise their faith and follow after the local gods.

God then allows the Israelites to be handed over to the local people groups in the land such as the Philistines and the Canaanites. These kings take total revenge on the Israelites because they were the ones that had invaded their land in the past. It was their right to place the Israelites

---

[1] http://www.jesusplusnothing.com/studies/images/cycle.gif

under harsh treatment. Slowly the Israelites begin to remember who they truly belong to and begin to call out seeking forgiveness. God, in mercy, then prepares a person to act as a judge and military leader to take the people and land back from their enemy. As we will see with the story of Deborah, God uses people with little might and a people with little to no power within themselves, but with God they prevail.

The consequence of their disobedience is that the Promised Land that Joshua and the other elders had conquered was now under the control of Jabin the Canaanite King. King Jabin placed his capital in Hazor, the northern part of the Israel. Hazor was about nine miles northwest of the Sea of Galilee. The capital was quite a distance from the main body of the Israelites. It was from here that he ruthlessly ruled the Israelites for twenty years.

In order to maintain the land he stationed a large military force at the base of Mount Carmel in the town of Harosheth hagoiim under the control of Commander Sisera. Sisera with his army of nine hundred iron clad chariots closed the trade routes which wound through the valley and plains. Those who traveled to trade goods were forced to take the narrow rocky hill paths so they could stay out of sight.

Under these harsh conditions the Israelites were forced to give up the land that their forefather had said ran with milk and honey. The fertile plains were abandoned and they fled to the mountaintops to make their living. The armies were also able to keep the Israelites from making and using weapons for their defense. The Israelites in their own strength had no power to fight back. Hungry and in poor conditions they finally called out to God for help. It was then that they began to repent of their ways and turned back to their worship of God.

Introduction to Deborah

Three thousand years later we are able to develop a clear picture of who this woman prophet, judge and warrior would have been. Israel had been under the control of King Jabin who held his court in Hazor. The Deuteronomic Historians, librarians of Hebrew literature during the Old Testament period, most likely placed within the text of Judges the name of the place where Deborah held her court. In the fourth chapter she is presented to the reader as the judge who sat under the Palm of Deborah.

Normally a judge would have held court near the gates that surrounded Jerusalem. Since the Israelites were forced to live in the hills above the plains, Deborah's court would also have been forced into the hills of Ephraim. Scripture places her court between Bethel and Ramah. This would have been seventy miles south of the Canaanite capital in Hazor and ten miles north of Jerusalem. The map on the next page gives some proportions to the hills and valleys. The drop from Bethel down to the Jericho is nearly three thousand feet.

Deborah must have wondered from time to time as she sat there looking off to the east about her nation's history. It was not that far back that, down in that valley, Joshua crossed the Jordon River to begin the conquest of the Promised Land. On a clear day she might have even been able to see where God had allowed Moses to peer into the land that he had led His chosen people to. These thoughts must have given her pause as she contemplated what to do with her different judgments.

Deborah, the wife of Lappidoth, was filled with the power of the Spirit of God. Her role as a prophetess for the people had become clear to all of her people who lived throughout Israel. Judges 5:7 calls her the "mother to all Israel." The scripture doesn't reveal if she and Lappidoth had any children of their own, but it is apparent that she earned the love of an entire nation.

Israel needed to have a mother at this time. The people who once knew what it meant to live on the fertile plains are now beginning to scratch out a living among the rocks. The elders of the group can look down onto the plains where their homes used to be. In fact, many looked down on the very families that at one time sat around their table for common meals.

24

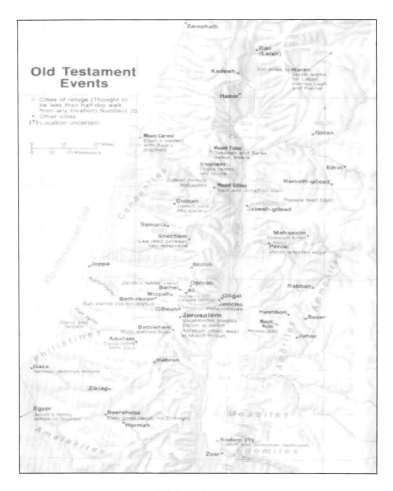

Biblestudy.org

They were beginning to feel the guilt that comes from turning your back on what you knew to be right and good. Growing up they could see the love their parents had for God as they would worship at the tabernacle. The many feasts throughout the year were designed to bring the Israelites closer to God and to each other. Unfortunately, after the death of Ehud, many did what was evil in the sight of their Lord. The temptations of the Canaanite culture lured them away from their God.

So it was that, as the people began to understand their spiritual and physical condition, they started to turn their hearts back to the one true God. It was under these palm trees that she was able to see the extraordinary needs of Israel as they were under the bondage of King Jabin. She knew of the promises God had given the Israelites[2] and most importantly she allowed herself to be used by God in this time of extreme trouble.

Deborah Hears the Word of the Lord

The book of Judges gives the reader two distinctly different styles in the accounting of Deborah and Barak's victory over the Canaanites. Chapter four is

---

[2] God chose the Israelite people to be priest and priestess to the world so that all may be saved. God made a covenant with Abraham that if he followed God faithfully his descendants would be more bountiful than the stars and sands on the beach. God continued to make this same covenant or promise with the Abraham's descendants. Again when the Israelites were in bondage in Egypt Moses was raised up from the wilderness to lead the chosen to freedom and the Promised Land. In the desert God again revealed the Glory of heaven to Moses and publicly made a covenant with the people of Israel.

strictly a chronological retelling of the story where the details are kept to a minimum. The fifth chapter is a poetic telling called The Song of Deborah. Many scholars believe this part of the Judges' manuscript to be one of the oldest recorded writings in all of scripture. This chapter is a victory song that most likely would have been written by Deborah. She would have sung this with help from a choir of women singers who were dedicated to this type of worship. Look for more information on the topic of women and music in this chapter's Bible Study.

Neither of the two chapters reports on how Deborah knew of the battle plans or the timing in which God was preparing to rescue the Israelite people. It is possible to let the text in verse four speak (4:4 NRSV) in that she is called a prophetess. Therefore, being a prophetess, she would have received messages and insight from God through some means. It may have been an angel or messenger or simply a vision from God. The text in chapter four simply states that Deborah sent a message to Barak for him to come to her.

Barak comes from the very region that is the location of the Canaanite capital where Jabin resides. The Lord is forcing the tribes of Naphtali and Zebulun to finish the task of defeating the Canaanite people in this region. It was because of their failure to obey that they were facing this formidable army.[3]

Barak must have been elated to be finally called into battle against Jabin. Jabin had made Barak's life miserable. In The Song of Deborah she recounts in verse eight that shields and spears were not to be found in large numbers among Barak's troops. At some point the Canaanites must have striped the Israelites of their weaponry. They may have done this through the battles that they won as they took the land away from the Israelites, or in the raids that followed.

Regardless of being without weapons, Deborah in her song praises the commanders that willingly came forward to do battle. The time had come when the leaders were again putting their faith and trust in the Lord that had taken care of them so many times in the past. They knew that God would give them victory over the Canaanites. They also placed their trust in the "mother of Israel" who had been guiding them.

Deborah instructs Barak to go back home so that he could rally his troops, and to also recruit members of the Zebulun tribe. Before Barak left to recruit the ten thousand

---

[3] Each of the twelve sons of Jacob became a tribe within the chosen people group known as the Israelites. Jacob was renamed Israel after the night that he wrestled with an angel of God. Each of the tribes was assigned an area in the Promised Land that they were to totally conquer by killing all of the inhabitants.

28

warriors he agreed to the mission only if she would go into battle with him. When she had heard Barak waiver with his desire to lead the troops into battle, she told him that he would not receive the glory of the battle, but it would be given over to a woman.

Barak went home to recruit the troops needed for battle. It would have seemed to be an impossible task to rally so many warriors since they had lost each encounter for the last twenty years. Farmers looked out to their fields to see what farming implements they could turn into weapons that could used against a fully fortified army. Shopkeepers, traders, and their sons came together with what they had and followed Barak to the top of Mount Tabor.

Each man that came out for battle came with an expectation that this would be a story to tell to their children's children. Expectation swelled each one with a sense of pride that they were willing to serve in God's army. If this were not true, they would have stayed home like the other Israelite tribes.

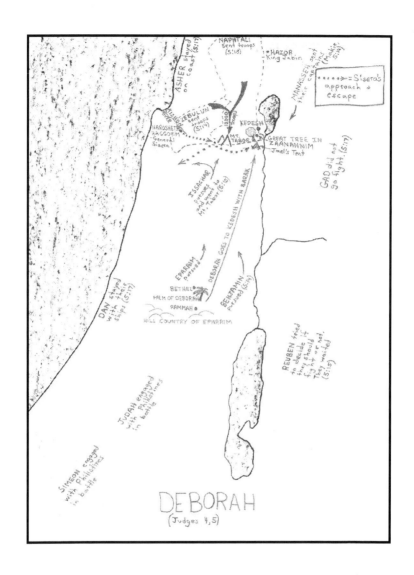

Unknown Author

Man Offers a Pitchfork & God Offers Thunder

If a Canaanite farmer had been working one of the fields in the Valley of Jezreel shown in the photo, he would have seen quite an event unfold before him. From his vantage point he could have viewed Sisera, the military commander of the Canaanite army, come charging through the valley from his base camp located at the bottom of Mount Carmel. The dust from their nine hundred iron clad chariots covered the battle-hardened foot soldiers that followed close behind.

The farmer could see that Sisera was heading directly towards Barak, the Israelite commander who was holding the high ground on Mount Tabor. This farmer would have expected to see another slaughter that day, because the small number of men on the mount was wearing the familiar battle gear that was common to a foot soldier. The farmer could see that these men were stationed in between the majority of the others who were holding sticks, rocks, and may even have had pitchforks.

The farmer had seen this before. The Israelites after being forced to leave their homes in the valleys would rally together to reclaim their homes and fields. Each time; though, the farmer had seen them leave the battlefield in defeat. In fact, the farmer was surprised that they hadn't given up on the dream of once again being the master of the land's that their "god" had given to them.

The farmer must have believed that their god, like his god, was just a myth. A belief to keep one focused on someone else fixing the problems that lay at hand. The farmer was accustomed to serving Baal who demanded many sacrifices so that the crops would grow and the rain would fall at their appropriate times.

This farmer who was enjoying the battle developing in front of him barely noticed that another band of soldiers was approaching from the south. This small diversionary force of soldiers was being led by their Prophetess and Judge Deborah. Deborah had recruited both the Ephraimites and the Benjaminites, who held the highlands directly south of the ensuing battle grounds.

Deborah could see across the flat plain that Sisera was closing in on Barak whose soldiers remained on the mount. Sisera's intention was to engage Barak on the valley floor where his chariots and their riders would quickly dispense this uprising. The spirit of the Lord caused Sisera to notice on his right the threat that was coming toward him from the city of Taanach. His military tacticians would have known this as a "pincher" maneuver.

A "pincher" is where two smaller forces trap a larger force between them. The troops in the middle of this are being attacked from both sides and it becomes easy to be distracted in battle. To avoid this trap Sisera turns his force directly into the path of Deborah. What the farmer on the plain and Sisera from his chariot couldn't see from their vantage points was that this battle developing in front of them was now going to be fought within the spiritual realm.

The sun that had been out all morning, drenching the heavily leather-clad soldiers in sweat, quickly disappeared behind the ominously black clouds that were forming. The temperature dropped suddenly, chilling everyone in the valley and on the hills. Pebbles began to clink together along the hardened pathways as they started to vibrate from the small tremors coming from deep within the earth.

The riders on the chariots were unaware of this first sign, but the foot soldiers on Mount Tabor had an inner feeling that Yahweh, their God, was about to again break forth in a miraculous presentation of monumental glory. Suddenly the mountains and the valley began to shake violently causing riders and soldiers from both armies to fall to the ground. Tremendous peals of thunder and bolts of lightning seared the air. Each person looked wildly around, seeking shelter or protection from the heavenly onslaught.

The farmer out in his field found himself alone. Looking across the valley as the tremors stopped he felt the first of the large raindrops. Soon these drops became a blinding wall of water causing the landscape to completely disappear. Later in Deborah's victory song, her song tells of how the Lord had left Seir and marched from the region of Edom to have the heavens and the cloud pour out the water onto the land.

The Israelite people would have understood that Seir is a realm of heaven. It is most likely that the farmer didn't understand that Sisera and the Canaanite soldiers were not only in a battle with Barak and Deborah, but also with the Creator of the universe. God, Yahweh, in Deborah's song is illustrated as a Mighty Warrior who uses the natural elements to wage combat against his enemies.

Out in the distance the farmer could hear the snorting, blowing and the pawing of the startled horses. Each time the thunder would clap the horses would strain against the tethers holding them to the chariots.

What the farmer couldn't see through the rain were the chariots becoming bogged down in the mud. The rain had come down so fast that the Kishon River and its tributary streams jumped their banks with flash floods causing the silt covering the land to turn immediately into a thick pasty mud.

Barak and Deborah seized upon the chaotic scene that played out before them. Together they converged onto the charioteers who couldn't get their chariots moving fast enough. This once domineering weapon was now nothing more than a three sided wall to hide behind. The Canaanite soldiers fled the battlefield. Barak and his warriors chased them all the way back to Harosheth hagoiim. Each of the

Canaanite soldiers that day fell by the very swords that they had left behind. Deborah and Barak knew that Yahweh had routed their enemy and had given them the battle. Deborah's Victory song is similar to the Song of the Sea[4] in that Yahweh is given the credit for swallowing up the chariots in a torrent of swirling water.

The Victory Goes to Jael

The great and mighty commander of the entire Canaanite army becomes so overwhelmed with fear that he leaps off his chariot and runs for the house of his ally, Heber the Kenite. Sisera no longer cared about his men who at this very moment were being slaughtered in battle; Sisera's only thought was for self-preservation.

The farmer that was in the valley that day is only a fictional figure that helps to develop a possible location of where Jael's husband was at the time of Sisera's death. It would be extremely interesting if the farmer that viewed the entire battle was in fact Heber the Kenite. At the very least this speculation doesn't take away from the true and actual events recorded in Judges four and five.

What is important to the text is who Heber was and where the Kenite tribe comes from. The Kenite tribe originally stems from Cain, the brother to Abel. Later this tribe is mentioned in association with Abram in the land of Canaan. Some scholarly works show that metalworking

---

[4] The Song of the Sea is credited to Merriam, the sister of Moses, after the victory over the Egyptians at the Reed Sea.

(bronze and iron) had come from this tribe. From this their metal smiths were able to help fashion musical instruments.[5]

Jethro, the father-in-law of Moses, a descendent of the Kenite tribe, was asked by Moses to travel with the Israelites to the Promised Land. The Kenites settled in the region around the city of Jericho. Later in scripture David uses them as scribes in the temple and they are incorporated into the tribe of Judah.[6]

Heber's clan; though, had broken away from their Israelite allegiance. Sisera knew that Heber was on friendly terms with King Jabin. Heber was living as a traitor against his fellow Israelites. He moved north from the Jericho area to live near those who held power at the time. Sisera felt that Heber's home would have been a safe haven from those who were chasing after him. What Sisera didn't consider is the idea that Heber's wife didn't hold to the same value system as her husband.

Sisera arrives weary from battle and from running for his life through the mud. Jael heard from her tent a man running in her direction that was apparently out of breath. She came out to meet this individual only to find that it was Sisera. Sisera was grateful that his friend's wife was at home.

---

[5] Jewishencyclepedia.com
[6] I Samuel 30:29 and 27:10

Jael heard from him the bizarre story of the battle that that had just unfolded in the valley. She could see the fear and bewilderment in his eyes. He kept nervously looking around waiting for one of the enemy warriors to jump out to finish him off. Sisera knew that in war the commander was a prize to be captured. It was commonplace to bring them back to the capital so they could be displayed as a trophy.

Jael comforted Sisera with her words and a promise that he would be safe with her. She led him into the tent where she had him lie down to rest. She covered him with

a warm blanket. Sisera asked Jael for a cup of water; he was parched from fear and his long flight. Jael had another thought in mind for him. She brought him a skin of warm milk and an ornate bowl of curds. The last words Sisera uttered were a plea for her to stand by the door to stand watch.[7]

Quickly the events of the day and the warm milk took their toll on Sisera. Now, it was Jael's role to pitch the tent wherever their nomadic tribe made camp. When

---

[7] Jael and Sisera" - by Gustav Dore (French artist, 1832-1883)

Jael knew that Sisera was sound asleep she crept toward him with the mallet she used to pitch her tent and an extra stake. She quickly placed the stake over Sisera's temple and skillfully drove the tent stake through his head. Sisera, the mighty commander, was killed by a woman just as Deborah had prophesied to Barak.

Barak finally found where Sisera had run off to and came to finish him off, but instead was met at the entrance to the tent by Jael. With a smile (or a smirk?), Jael offered Barak to enter her tent where he saw Sisera pegged to the tent floor.

Barak knew that his job was not finished with this one battle. He took his warriors who now were fully armed with the spoils of war and went forward to finish the conquest of King Jabin. The tide had turned, and again the Israelites began to reestablish their claim upon the land. Finally, after putting many hardships on King Jabin, they destroyed him and his empire.

Yahweh intervened again so that the Israelites would again turn their hearts toward their God. Yahweh used the natural elements of this world to accomplish this. Look around each day to see just how God is working in your life.

MONDAY

FINDING YOUR WAY OUT OF THE SPIN CYCLE

Joshua and his fellow Israelites failed to completely obey God's instruction in removing those people groups that lived in their Promised Land. In this chapter Stephen discussed the "sin cycle" the Israelites found themselves in. The Bible reveals to us still today various commands given to us from God on how we need to need to emphasize certain thoughts and actions in our lives.

Reflect on this and allow the Holy Spirit to remind you what some of these actions may be. Here are some positive commands that you can use: Matthew 5:43-46, Luke 12:33-40.

Throughout the book of Judges the writer reveals their disobedience concerning the act of intermarriage with those other than Israelites. This led them into various degrees of compromise where they began adopting other people's customs. Because of their intermarriage they were more willing to follow after the worship of Baal.

What compromises do we allow in our lifestyle and relationships when we fail to cut from our lives those things contrary to God's purpose?

TUESDAY

WANTED: WOMEN SONG LEADERS

PLEASE APPLY

Carol Meyers, in her book "Exodus", closely examines the role women play as composers and performers of music in the Israelite culture where the music has been well-developed and has a high level of sophistication.[8] Secular and religious events were augmented by those who danced, played musical instruments and sang. It doesn't take one long when reading the Old Testament to see the rich language used to describe the various instruments and to hear musical terms.

It is through passages like the one where Miriam sings a victory song (Exodus 15:1-21), or where Deborah sings her victory song here in Judges, that many begin to see the important role women have had in this culture. This belief is also corroborated through archaeology. Many little statues depict women playing the drums which were essential for most musical performances to keep the beat.

How do you feel about women today being part of ministry? Have we gotten to the point where we acknowledge and accept a woman's calling to ministry?

---

[8] Meyer, Carol. Exodus. Cambridge University Press. 2005. Pg.114

Wednesday

Comparison of Two Armies

Canaanite	Israelite
Seasoned leader with a winning record	Seasoned leader with a losing record
Well trained soldiers	Farmers and shepherds
900 Iron Clad Chariots	Pitchforks, stones and clubs
Hadad, the storm god	Yahweh, creator God

Compare the information given above. If you were a person willing to make a prediction prior to their conflict in the valley of Jezreel, which army would you have picked to win?

After reading the chapter, what allowed the Israelites to carry the battle? Who truly won the victory?

Yahweh used a storm to confuse the soldiers and to startle the horses. Isn't it interesting that Yahweh would use the very instrument, the storm, of the Canaanite's god to cause them to fail in their conquest?

THURSDAY

A MIGHTY WARRIOR?

Sisera	Barak
Self Confident	Insecure
Faith in swords/chariots	Faith in Deborah
Faith in his training	Dependent on others
Strong leader	Weak leader

These are the two warriors that went into battle and one lost the battle and his life. One was a natural born leader and had the victories to prove it. The other knew that he was unable to carry the day without help. Yahweh worked a miracle through Barak's willingness to follow Deborah into the battle.

We often look at Barak as not being willing to take the lead, but we fail to understand that he was still faithful to the task at hand. Even through his weaknesses and inabilities God was still able to use him for God's glory.

Has God ever used one of your weaknesses to bring blessings to someone else?

FRIDAY

ARE YOU A RELUCTANT WARRIOR TOO?

How do you view yourself today? Do you feel like "a Barak" in that you are not capable of doing for God what He is expecting of you? Well, it is possible that you may not be able to, yet with God's help you will become victorious, regardless of your abilities.

Are you willing to accept the challenge of serving God through the weak areas in your life?

Barak and Deborah faced a physical battle and God fought the battle with nature's fury. Are you willing to allow God to help you fight your battles in unorthodox ways?

Are you willing to let others take the victory lap so that God can receive the glory and praise?

"Gideon thanks God for the miracle of the dew", painting by Maarten van Heemskerck (Musée des Beaux-Arts de Strasbourg), *Gédéon* (vers 1550),

Yahweh's intervention through "Deceitful Stratagems"

Gideon

From Winnowing to Testing To Victory

Historical Setting

Gideon's story as a judge over Israel begins in the sixth chapter with Israel again doing what they see as right, but which is evil in the sight of the Lord. Gideon's story ends in chapter eight with his death. These three chapters reveal to the reader that God, Yahweh, had remained faithful to the Covenant that was made with Abraham and his descendants. These three chapters also reveal the mysterious method of choosing the least likely candidate, who finds himself in a seemingly unwinnable situation: to complete God's ordained mission.

Chapter five ends with a simple statement that again confirms the cycle the Israelites find themselves in. The people who lived in the Promised Land had experienced peace for forty years. Entering into chapter six the Lord is handing the Israelites over to the rule of the Midianites. It seems that the lessons learned by one generation are not easily passed onto the next generation. The story of Gideon reveals the one key sin that caused Yahweh to allow for the destruction of the twelve tribes of Israel. The town, including Gideon's family, had built altars to the god Baal.

Slowly, over time, the temptations began to pull the Israelites away from their true God. These temptations stem back to the sin of Joshua.

Judges 2:19-23 (NRSV) *"But whenever the judge died, they would relapse and behave worse than their ancestors, following other gods, worshiping them and bowing down to them. They would not drop any of their practices or their stubborn ways. So the anger of the LORD was kindled against Israel; and he said, "Because this people have transgressed my covenant that I commanded their ancestors, and have not obeyed my voice, I will no longer drive out before them any of the nations that Joshua left when he died." In order to test Israel, whether or not they would take care to walk in the way of the LORD as their ancestors did, the LORD had left those nations, not driving them out at once, and had not handed them over to Joshua."*

Joshua failed to follow the command given to him by God to remove the people from the land. It bears repeating that it is from this failure to obey that after each time God comes to their rescue they again are tempted by the people who are native to the land. It is their culture that seduces the carnal nature of the Israelites' base character. The Israelites are continually being drawn in because they refuse to remain faithful. The two people groups begin again to share with each other and begin to intermarry. It is from these unions that the Israelites are being compromised from within.

Baal Worship

Very little was known of the Canaanite pantheon of which Baal is the preeminent god(s). The Old Testament had been the primary source to study the culture that surrounded the god(s) Baal. There are eighty-nine direct references to Baal; the goddess Asherah is mentioned forty times; ten time the goddess Ashtoreth is referenced. The Old Testament text makes note of the various places in which the people worshiped these gods. It also makes known that the people used statues and sacred poles as part of their worship practice.

Archaeologists were able to collaborate much of the Old Testament text with the identification of places of worship where temples, smaller shrines along and open-air sanctuaries were located. Many of these sites can be found on a map of the Old Testament. Some of the various sites are: Megiddo on the Jezreel plain, Zorah, Lachish, Ai, and

Beth-shan. Many of these sites have surrendered up to professional excavators objects that were used in worship. These items include libation bowls, pottery incense stands, and steles representing the various deities.

The most significant city to be excavated was Ugarit. It was discovered when a peasant farmer out plowing his field inadvertently pulled up a flagstone covering the entrance to a burial chamber.[9] It was here that thousands of texts have been found and recovered.[10] These texts were on clay tablets that were dated back to 1400 to 1200 BCE.[11] There were several different languages represented, some of which were Egyptian, Hittite, Sumerian and one previously unknown language.

---

[9] http://bible.org/article/baalism-canaanite-religion-and-its-relation-selected-old-testament-texts.See Pfeiffer, *Ras Shamra and the Bible,* 9-18; Michael David Coogan, ed. and trans., *Stories from Ancient Canaan* (Philadelphia: Westminster Press, 1978), 10-11; G. R. Driver, *Canaanite Myths and Legends,* Old Testament Series, vol. 3 (Edinburgh: T & T Clarke, 1956), 1.

[10] http://bible.org/article/baalism-canaanite-religion-and-its-relation-selected-old-testament-texts. In a discussion with K. Lawson Younger, Jr., (Feb. 1997) he stated that there have been at least 500 more texts discovered at Ras Shamra since 1993-95. Apparently these were all in Ugaritic, date from 1400-1200 B. C. E., and represent a wide variety of genres including sacerdotal traditions. Unfortunately, very few have been published.

[11] http://bible.org/article/baalism-canaanite-religion-and-its-relation-selected-old-testament-texts. Johannes C. De Moor, *An Anthology of Religious Texts from Ugarit,* Religious Texts Translation Series, ed. M. S. H. G. Heerma Van Voss, et al, vol. 16 (Leiden: E. J. Brill, 1987), viii.

It was the unknown text that ultimately provides the best information concerning the Canaanite Pantheon. The language was named "Ugaritic" after the city in which the tablets were found, Ugarit. At the time these tablets were produced the city of Ugarit must have been a flourishing city that conducted business on an international level. These tablets have become known as the Ras Shamra Texts. These texts corroborate much of what is written in the Old Testament. The practices regarding Baal that are denounced in the Bible are also found within the Ras Shamra Texts.

There seem to be many similarities to the known system of Greek gods. The texts refer to a Baal Cycle in which the universe revolves around a political reality which connects on three different levels. First, Baal's rule extends to the cosmic where the many deities interact. The second level is where the political events reflect a concern for human society. The last level is where Baal or the gods use nature's natural phenomena such as lightning, thunder and rains to demonstrate their power.

The major concern at this point is to understand the word "Baal" in the context of the Old Testament. It is extremely important to understand that Baal is a generic word used as a title. In its most simple form it means "master" or "lord." Just as in the Hebrew culture, they were to refrain from using the Lord's name, so the Baal worshipers had other names to replace their god's name. The Canaanite priest used the term Baal in association with their various gods. In later writings Baal became closely associated with the god Hadad, or the "storm god". In all, there were over fifteen gods that used the name Baal.[12]

In the Canaanite Pantheon the first god was known as "El". El was the creator and the father of the other gods. Asherah is referred to the mother of the gods. She shared in the work of El. These gods had their roles within the cycle of the year and with the land. The people of Canaan felt that they had to appease these gods for the rain to fall in its season, for their crops to grow, for their own ability to conceive and, in general, for all aspects of their daily life.

In many ways the two cultures easily blend with each other. The Israelites had two major disadvantages living in the Promised Land during the time of the Judges. First, their God, Yahweh, did not allow any images to be made for worship. It seems that our nature wants to have the comfort of seeing the physical representation. Whatever the reasoning, humanity has trouble accepting the spirit world. The Hebrews experienced this in the midst of their departure from Egypt. While Moses was on the mountain speaking with God, his brother Aaron built the golden calf. The second disadvantage is that the majority of what would become the Old Testament had yet to occur. The priest had at that time just bits and pieces of the Torah

---

[12] http://bible.org/article/baalism-canaanite-religion-and-its-relation-selected-old-testament-texts

(Genesis, Exodus, Leviticus, Numbers, and Deuteronomy) written down.

This subject will be further discussed in the weekly study materials. Here you will explore the practical problems we face in today's culture.

The Prophet is Sent

God's chosen children have slipped away again. This time they had fallen to a new low. They had lived for forty years in peace with God, once again on the valley floors where they were able to see the benefits from their labor. However, just like their parents and grandparents that fought alongside of Barak and Deborah, they again found themselves living in caves and among the clefts of the rocks on the high mountains.

The Midianites[13] held true to their name which in Hebrew means strife or contention. The Lord God allowed them to enter into the Promised Land to take full advantage

---

[13] Genesis 25:1-6 Abraham took another wife, whose name was Keturah. She bore him Zimran, Jokshan, Medan, Midian, Ishbak, and Shuah. Jokshan was the father of Sheba and Dedan. The sons of Dedan were Asshurim, Letushim, and Leummim. The sons of Midian were Ephah, Epher, Hanoch, Abida, and Eldaah. All these were the children of Keturah. Abraham gave all he had to Isaac. But to the sons of his concubines Abraham gave gifts, while he was still living, and he sent them away from his son Isaac, eastward to the east country.

of the various seasons--and they didn't just enter the land; they stormed it, like a plague of locust. Their numbers were so numerous that it was impossible to count the men and their camels. The Midianites overtook all of the land and in the process the crops were destroyed along with the sheep, cattle and donkeys.

There entrance into the land also sent a signal to the Amalekites and other eastern nations that the land of Israel was open to be ravaged. For seven years the Midianites and Amalekites covered the land. At some point during their occupation, the Israelites began to cry out to God. God heard their cry and sent them a prophet to challenge them by reminding them of their past. The prophet also confronted them on their disobedience concerning following after other gods and not listening to the voice of God.

The Call of Gideon (as seen by his father)

Let me, Joash from the clan Abiezrite and the tribe of Manasseh, tell you the story of my son Gideon as a proud father would do. Gideon comes from a long, long, long line of a people full of pride. He comes by it naturally, ever since our ancestor Abram left the land of Ur. I have come to believe that there are only three things we have been able to count on: our God, our families, and our pride.

Our people have been on the move since Ur. Sure, we always had a promise that this land would be ours, but it seems that as soon as we obtain it the hope and dream slips away like the sand I hold here in my hand, slowly sifting away between my fingers.

It was here in this land that Abram received the grand vision that his descendants would populate the land like the grains of sand that cover the seashore or like the uncountable stars filling the heavens.[14] The problem with that vision is that we didn't include Abram's other offspring, our distant cousins the Midianites, who are now overtaking our land down in the valleys.

Our cousins have been let loose by God to again punish us for our various sins. I know that I have not been as faithful to Yahweh as I should have been. In fact, it was through the angel of the Lord that I lost my sacred shrine to Baal, the storm god. Now I am getting somewhat ahead of my son's grand story.

Let me go back a little so that I can to tell you why we have come naturally to always being on the move. Abram left a land full of wealth to travel here. He had no home. So you might call him and all of us Israelites, nomads. You see, our ancestors made their living by raising livestock that consisted of sheep, oxen, and camels.

---

[14] Genesis 22:17

Look around this land and you will see that it is full of green pastures and mounds of rocks.

Since Abram moved here, we have had to fight the local inhabitants continuously for places for our livestock to graze. Many skirmishes have been fought over the wells just so that we could water our stock. I think that maybe, just maybe, that is why we have not been as concerned about moving to the mountains as we should have been. We have not put down our roots into the ground that Yahweh has given to us. But enough of an old man thinking back to how we got here; it is more important to let you know how we got out of this terrible situation.

Like I said before, my Gideon became a leader of the entire nation even though we come from the weakest clan in the Manasseh tribe. I don't like to think about it, but it is true that Gideon was also the weakest in our clan. It seems that life at the bottom of the barrel prepared Gideon for the tasks that were going to confront him, and later on perhaps, it was part of the undoing of his achievements.

It seems from my experience as a lifelong herder of sheep that the runts of a litter are sometimes the best fighters despite their size. They have the most to prove to themselves and to the world. Gideon, born last into this family and clan, had much to prove. I think that is why he was always so industrious and always using his head.

Gideon's call as I understand it came one night as he was down in the bottom of a pit that at one time had been a winepress, threshing out the wheat that we were able to get ahold of. My son was smart enough do this task out of the sight of those Midianites. If they knew he had found this grain, I am sure that they would have stolen it back from us.

So there was Gideon working his heart out and I assume that he was tired and wanted to take a break or something. Now the angel of the Lord had come and sat down next to the old oak tree by Ophrah. Here is where my father's pride wells up and the hair sticks straight out on my old arms. Gideon was passing by this tree and that angel calls out to him with a strange greeting; "The Lord is with you, you mighty warrior."

I don't know where my son gets his brashness from (maybe it's his mother), but he answers the angel with a question. Gideon, with a polite smile, asks that if the Lord is with us, then why are we living as we do and the Midianites are allowed to take away our lands? We have heard the stories around our campfires, he said, of all of the wonderful deeds that the Lord has done and how he had cared for us in Egypt, and even brought us out of that horrible place. Yet, here we are living as the Lord's cast-offs.

The angel did not answer this question, but instead turned my son's righteous anger into a constructive command. This angel (whom I think was truly the Lord) tells my son Gideon to go with the strength he had within himself to deliver Israel from the Midianites. The Lord went on to actually commission him right then and there.

Gideon, not the most trusting fellow, asked for a sign. He asked that the Lord would stay long enough so that he could bring him a present of cakes and meat. I think that Gideon needed time to take it all into his head that the Lord was actually calling him out to act. The Lord consented and stayed till Gideon returned.

Gideon brought out the food in a basket. The angel commanded Gideon to place the basket on a rock. He then said to pour the broth out over the basket, the meat and the flour cakes. It was then that the Lord touched the basket and suddenly--may the Lord be praised!--there was fire shooting up from the rock and it consumed it all. At that moment the Lord simply vanished. Gideon called out "Help me, Lord God! I have seen you face to face." Now I don't know if Gideon simply heard it in his head or the Lord actually called through the mist of the evening, but our Lord answered and said, "Peace be to you and be not afraid for you shall not die." Right then and there, just as our forefathers had done, Gideon built an altar that still stands today. We have called this altar "The Lord is Peace".

Gideon Tears Down Baal's Altar

Hold on, since I am just getting started with my son's tale. That very night Gideon was also commanded by God to tear down his family's altar that was erected to honor the gods of Baal.

Now, let me remind you that this was *my* altar. I have to say that I was responsible for leading my clan away from the true worship of Yahweh. The Lord had to deal first with the sin in our life before Gideon would have the power to deal with the entire nation. I guess that I knew that in my heart. So when the members of our clan came to me the next morning with the news that Baal's altar was broken down, with the sacred pole being used to burn a bull on it, I defended my son's actions.

They were so angry with Gideon that they wanted me to hand him over to them so that they could kill him. Maybe some of the Lord's command fell on me that day. I was able to find relief in my heart from the sins that I had committed before the Lord and told all those in my clan that if Baal was so powerful then let Baal take care of himself. In fact, I got a little righteous anger going myself, and challenged them that if they stood up for Baal then they would be put to death by the next morning.

Now, I know how important names are to our people. So, I changed the name of Gideon that day to Jerubbaal, which means "Let Baal challenge him." Our house and our clan that day were finally right before our Lord and God. Now this is where the story begins to get good. It was at that same time that the Midianites and others from the east crossed the Jordon River to camp in the Valley of Jezreel. The very spirit of the Lord entered Gideon. He sounded the trumpet to call others to follow him into battle. Our clan was the first to respond.

Messengers were sent out to the various tribes. First, they went to the members of Manasseh, our tribe. Our tribe was given the land on both sides of the Jordon River so it only makes sense that we respond first. My son also knew that we were not strong enough on our own, so those other messengers went on to those who fought in the last war against the Canaanites; those who lived in Asher, Zebulun and Naphtali came to meet with my son.

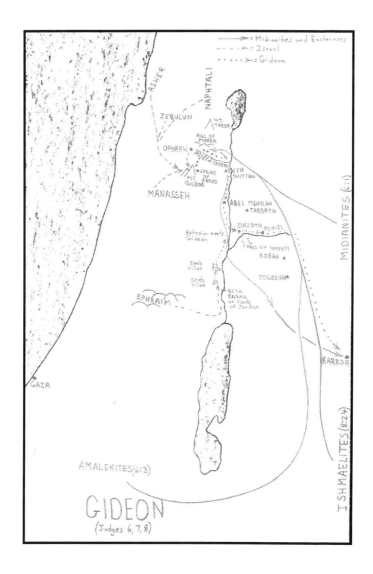

Author unknown

Gideon: Not the Most Trusting Fellow

Gideon was concerned that he would be going into a futile battle and wanted to make sure that Yahweh was with him. Now I mentioned before that my son was not the most trusting person. So, before he committed himself and all of his fellow countrymen, he called out to God with a request. I thought that the first one was really easy to accomplish. He set out a piece of sheep's wool on the stone floor where he was threshing the wheat. The test for God was to have the wool saturated with water and the floor around it should remain dry.

Sure enough the next day when he got up he was able to wring out a full bowl of water from the dew. Now, I am not sure that I would have asked God for a second test, but Gideon was determined to see if Yahweh would stand with him in battle. So Gideon asked the Lord to do just the opposite the next night. It so happened that the wool was completely dry while the flagstones were slippery with the night's dew.

All Praise Goes to Yahweh for the Victory

Now, I know that I have told you some tales that seem to be farfetched. Please indulge an old man with one more story that will make all the others seem insignificant. My God truly is to be praised for what was accomplished through my son Gideon.

Gideon took his forces to camp near the Harod springs. Now here I am to tell you how proud I am of my son. Over thirty-two thousand men and boys came out to fight with my son. Can you imagine? Gideon, the weakest of all of our clans, a leader of these warriors of God!

I am sure that many of you know where this is, but if not, these springs are in the hills that are just southeast of the Jezreel valley. The beginning part of the floor on this valley is the most northern part of our tribe's territory. It was from this high ground that Gideon's troops could see the campfires of the Midianites. They were about five miles to the north at the base of the hill of Moreh.

Now, Gideon must have been completely knocked off his rock when the Lord called out to him saying, "Gideon, the troops are too many. If you win with all of them then they could say that they did it on their own and would not learn to follow me. This is a lesson that I want my people to learn. So, here is the new plan. Gather the troops and let them know that if any one of them is trembling because they are full of fear they are free to go home without guilt."

If it had been me I know that I would have felt my heart sink down to the bottom of my dirty sandals. Here my son looked around him to find ten thousand men left. He watched as twenty-two thousand fearful men left for home. What a feeling of loss. Yet God wasn't finished with Gideon.

Yahweh again called to Gideon. "The number is still too high." At this Gideon looked back across the valley to where the Midianites were camped. He knew from the scouts that reported back to him that there were over one hundred thirty-five thousand well-armed soldiers waiting for the trumpet call to lead them into battle.

Yahweh had Gideon lead his troops down to the water to drink. While at the water's edge Gideon was to watch how the men drank. I want you to know this, that God was putting the men to a test. Gideon knew this, but they did not. If they had known then they would have tried to beat it so that they could be part of the team that attacked their enemy.

I think God has an interesting way of picking the smallest, the weakest and in some cases the not so bright. Out of the ten thousand that were left three hundred got down on their bellies and drank like a dog. If you are not part of our culture maybe you don't know that we don't like dogs. They are useless and disgusting.

So guess who God chooses to go into battle with my son? The nine thousand plus who were good soldiers who stayed alert, looking for the enemy while reaching down and cupping the water to drink from their hands, or those lazy men that drank like a dog? You guessed it: the three hundred. God was on a mission to prove once and for all that the nation of Israel needed to place their full trust in their God who delivers.

Now the Lord God said to my son: "With these three hundred I will deliver the Midianites into your hand. Now, take from the others their clay jars and their trumpets and then send them home." That night the Lord knew my son's heart and his distrust, so he allowed Gideon to go over by the cover of darkness to hear the dreams being discussed by their soldiers. So it was that Gideon took with him Purah his servant and they crossed the valley where an outpost was set up.

I need you to see what Gideon saw that night. He crossed over a valley that was filled with the campfires of one hundred thirty thousand men. The valley was lit up from one end to the other. The fires were close together as well to accommodate so many people.

When Gideon slithered near one outpost a man was telling the others around the campfire the dream that had just awakened him. Gideon heard him tell of a cake of barley bread that tumbled into their camp and turned over their tents. (Remember my son in the pit threshing the wheat.) One of the other soldiers, with a little panic in his voice, said that it must be the sword of Gideon, son of Joash. I like that he added me into this part of the prophet's answer. He went on to say that God had given them over to the Israelites.

Silently Gideon worshiped Yahweh right then and there. He now knew in his heart that the battle would be given to him. Gideon was filled with the power of the Lord's spirit and it propelled him back across the valley. Upon entering his own camp he yelled for everyone to get up. "The Lord has delivered the Midianites into our hands!"

Gideon divided his group into three companies and put a trumpet into each of the hands of those that were left. These were the trumpets that he had collected from the squad leaders that went on home. He also gave each one a jar so they could put a torch in it.

Let me pull you aside here to let you know a little of God's strategy. In our day the leader or the commander would be the one to have carried the trumpet and a torch. It was with this method that the Midianite soldiers would have thought the Israelite army to be massive.

Before they headed out to find their positions, Gideon gave them clear instructions on what to do after blowing the trumpets and breaking the pots. They were to scream as loud as they could, "For the Lord and for Gideon."

So, it was a proud night for me as Gideon and his little band of three hundred men left their camp to do battle for the Lord. Gideon had planned that at the start of the middle watch, and when the Midianite soldiers had finished switching the guards, they would attack. It was easy to see the switching of the guards with the number of campfires still burning.

It was at that moment that Gideon took his clay pot and broke it open, setting in motion the battle. Each one of his troops followed Gideon's example. They broke their pots and the flames jumped up towards the sky and the torches sucked in the fresh oxygen. They took their trumpets and blew them as loud and long as they could. Next, the entire company almost in unison yelled out; "A sword for the Lord and for Gideon."

Gideon's men's hearts began to pound as they watched the terror of their enemies unfold before them. Men came running out of their tents confused and disorientated. They began to swing their swords at anything that moved in front of them. The Midianites attacked each other throughout the night with cries of fear of both the Israelite's God and of Gideon. As the dawn began to appear they saw what they were doing to each other and began to flee away from the battle.

Gideon sent those three hundred men back to their homes where their fellow clansmen were. Now they all were invited to chase after the Midianites as they were fleeing. Men came from Ephraim and as far as Bethbarah and the Jordon. Together they captured many, but they killed the two leaders Oreb and Zeeb.

Now, there is more to the story, but I am old and will let someone else bring this to you. Or maybe you could read chapter eight on your own to see how my son let his ego get in his way. I will say this: that he lived to be an old man himself and had seventy sons.

One last thing to know: the Midianites did not raise their heads again. They knew that they had been conquered. The land was at rest for forty years because of what my son had done.

I learned from the story of my son that God can use a simple strategy to confuse the enemy. We don't have to be large in number, but we do have to be willing to allow God to use our weaknesses for God's glory.

MONDAY

PUTTING YOUR HOUSE IN ORDER

God called Gideon to remove the Midianites from the territories of Israel. Before Gideon was fully released to conquer Israel's enemy, God had one last detail for Gideon to take care of: Gideon had to set his house in order by removing all the symbols of the foreign gods. He had to set the example of living a life that was holy and set apart for God before he could fulfill Yahweh's command to strike down the Midianites.

God is calling on you today to conquer the world by offering hope to others through sharing with them the message of the Good News. Just as Gideon had been reluctant to openly sanctify his home, what have you been hesitating or reluctant to remove from your life or your home so that you are living a holy lifestyle?

Gideon was fearful to make that first move of cutting down the family altar. He waited until the cover of darkness to so his work might be done in secret. God didn't scold Gideon for being afraid. God knows that we are fearful and weak of heart. Is there something you believe God wants you to do, but you are afraid of your family's reaction? Would you be tempted to act for God if you knew it could be kept as a secret?

TUESDAY

SIN AND HABITS REAR THEIR HEAD

In this story Gideon finds the Midianites as his adversary. In this chapter we learned that the Midianites were the descendents of Abraham. Abraham was remarried to Keturah after his wife, Sarah, passed away. Together they had a son whom they named Midian[15]. The Midianites became a people known for their tricks and treachery: they were the traders who had bought and sold Joseph into slavery in Egypt. Moses was obedient to God when he was told to fully defeat the Midian people.[16] The Midianites were carelessly allowed to live on the fringes of their communities where their tricks and treachery could continuously infect and subvert the Israelites. The Midianites are again being used by God to bring the Israelites back to holy living.

This is an example of what can happen in our own lives when we carelessly allow our temptations and sinful habits to hang around on the fringes. We may think that once we have conquered these sins and habits that we don't have to stay vigilant. In truth, we must always be aware of those things that trigger our desires to walk in areas that lead us into sin.

---

[15] Genesis 25:2
[16] Numbers 25:16-18 & 31:1-9

WEDNESDAY

TO FLEECE OR NOT TO FLEECE

Gideon had a command given to him by God. Gideon used a fleece for spiritual confirmation of this command; the fleece method is not a cavalier way to seek directions or instructions on how to live your life. The task set out before him was huge and overwhelming. Gideon wanted to get it right the first time.

Gideon's test was also one that would not happen naturally, but only through the supernatural intervention from God. This seems natural since God was asking Gideon to expect the supernatural.

Has God called you to a specific task that has overwhelmed you? (Write it out here so it is clearly defined.)

If you have an idea that God is calling you to a specific action and you are unsure if this is from God or from your own desire, create a fleece that will confirm God's desire for you. Go forth and conquer that which has been given to you.

THURSDAY

WEAK AND WEAKER STILL

Have you ever felt that you were so fully prepared for an upcoming personal test that you heard yourself saying; "I've got this one under control." This could have been Gideon when all of his troops showed up to fight. It would have been easy to say; "Hey, we've got this one in the bag."

The question for you then is this: who gets the glory, you or God? In truth, who gave you the abilities to complete the personal test?

They all came from God, not one of us has ever been a self-made person.

Many times people are brought down from those lofty mountains of self-reliance to a point where they can only look up for help. It is here in these moments of self-realization that we surrender ourselves to our Creator and find the strength and courage to move forward. It is also in those times that events seem to work out that were totally out of our control.

What has God worked in your life when you were at your weakest?

Friday

Testing Those Who are Unaware

Gideon called his men over to the springs where they could drink. No other directions were given to these men or an explanation of why they were drinking. Many of those who had been in battle before knew how one could become dehydrated from their physical exertion. This command of getting something to drink would have been a natural order from a commanding officer. In truth, this was a test to see who would be eligible for the battle.

If there is one thing we have learned about God, there is a sense of consistency evidenced throughout God's holy word. God shows over and over again patience with the children of Israel. God offers grace when we least deserve it. God uses those who are weak to do great things. God lifts up the underdog.

So, with God's consistency in mind doesn't it make sense that still today God allows us to live out normal events that are actually tests for us?

What do you do when you drive by someone with a sign asking to work for food? Have you thought of letting someone cut in front of you in the checkout line at the grocery store? Do you turn the radio off when a song began to play that is not consistent with God's values?

72

Samson destroys the temple of Dagon, 1890 Bible illustration

Yahweh's intervention through "Lustful Desires"

Sampson

The Judge who throws temper tantrums

Historical Setting

The opening verse of chapter thirteen brings us back once again to the fact that Israel falls into the temptation of sin and begins to perform acts that are evil in the sight of the Lord. In the story of Samson the nation of Israel as a whole reaches their lowest level of separation from God.

The land of Israel had surely seen its share of battles where the blood of many had been spilt. Each time Israel had to face a new adversary their young sons and men would march off to fight for their freedom. In each of the conflicts, the price of life was high. After all those years it becomes understandable why they began to lose heart.

Life for the Israelites before the birth of Sampson was again full of hardship. The Philistines moved up from the coastline in southern Judah to occupy much of the mountains and valley all the way to the Jordon River. From time to time the Amorites would send raiding parties from the east and cross over the Jordon River to engage in warfare.

Since the forty years of rest under Gideon as their judge, the Israelites had several judges that tried to bring them under the full authority of Yahweh. Instead, the Israelites clung to their cycle of disobedience and fell deeper and deeper into their sins. Sin becomes a strange master as we will see in the story of Sampson. Sin takes us to places we never would dream of going. Sin keeps us in places longer than we ever dreamed of staying.

This stickiness of sin had completely invaded the character of the Israelites by the time Sampson was conceived. Their despair and despondency becomes realized since they had been under the oppression of the Philistines for forty years. In the previous years the nation as a whole would call out to God for relief and for forgiveness of what they had become. They desired God to intervene in their lives so that they again could be in God's presence. This time the text does not bring them to this point. Chapter thirteen reveals their sin, the occupation of the Philistines and the actions of a loving God who reaches out to a couple who has remained faithful.

Sampson's setting for his story has moved from the middle and northern part of Israel to the southern regions. Both Gideon and Barak fought most of their major battles in the Jezreel Valley. The scene in which Sampson stars is located mainly in the tribal territories of Dan and Judah.

After an extremely short introduction in verse one the angel of the Lord appeared to a woman who had been barren throughout her marriage to Manoah from the tribe of Dan. The Lord moved directly to the point in scripture and informed this unnamed wife of Manoah that she would bear a son. The Lord also made some strong demands on her. She was to avoid wine or any strong drink and not to eat anything unclean according to the Mosaic Law prior to her conception and while she carried their son.

Sampson is to be a Nazirite

There were three characters in the Bible that lived a Nazirite lifestyle; Sampson, Samuel, and John the Baptist. Each of these gentlemen had at least one main thing in common: the mothers of these three men were all barren, and they each had a special revelation or message from God that their sons would be set aside from birth to perform a special function. There are three specific requirements to be a true Nazirite. Moses is given instructions from God in Numbers to explain what the requirements are to be.

Numbers 6:1-8 (NRSV) *"The LORD spoke to Moses, saying: Speak to the Israelites and say to them: When either men or women make a special vow, the vow of a nazirite to separate themselves to the LORD, they shall separate themselves from wine and strong drink; they shall drink no wine vinegar or other vinegar, and shall not drink any grape juice or eat grapes, fresh or dried. All their days as nazirites they shall eat nothing that is produced by the grapevine, not even the seeds or the skins. All the days of their nazirite vow no razor shall come upon the head; until the time is completed for which they separate themselves to the LORD, they shall be holy; they shall let the locks of the head grow long. All the days that they separate themselves to the LORD they shall not go near a corpse. Even if their father or mother, brother or sister, should die, they may not defile themselves; because their consecration to God is upon the head. All their days as nazirites they are holy to the LORD."*

Manoah's wife, during her pregnancy, was also commanded to live a Nazirite lifestyle. The entire purpose of these three actions is not performing a mystical act, but to have an external expression of being set aside for the work of the Lord. We, who have been baptized, in essence, live out the same experience. Our lives are set aside to be holy just as Sampson was. Baptism and being a nazirite are outward expressions of an inward covenant that God has made with us and for us. Sampson was set aside for the work of the Lord even while he was in his mother's womb.

The Lord also made a special comment concerning the birth of Sampson. This future judge would begin to deliver the Israelites from the Philistines. In other words, Sampson will **only start the process of removing** these foreigners from their Promised Land. This is the first time that the Lord did not offer to totally free them from their enemy. One can only assume the reason for this new method of dealing with these stiff-necked people. It is possible that they had traveled too far this time into their sin nature. It was time that they had more external control placed on their daily living. It was time for a kingdom.

The Angel of the Lord Confirms the Message

The wife of Manoah seeks to find her husband after receiving this strange yet hopeful message. Her world had just spun around completely. She had been living her whole life in disgrace for her inability to have children. Women in general were not held in high regard. Human nature in the women of the time was to pick on those who were weaker than themselves. Now Sampson's mother would have the upper hand. She had had a personal word from the Lord that her son would be a Nazirite, set aside for work that was holy and honoring to God.

You can just see her running all over the camp looking for Manoah. When she finally finds him she is out of breath and most likely speaking so fast at Manoah tries to calm her down. He must be wondering if she had too much to the wine or some other strong drink to make her act so strange.

Listen to her trying to give him the good news in one long burst.

Judges 13:6 (NIV) *Then the woman went to her husband and told him, "A man of God came to me. He looked like an angel of God, very awesome. I didn't ask him where he came from, and he didn't tell me his name. But he said to me, 'You will conceive and give birth to a son. Now then, drink no wine or other fermented drink and do not eat anything unclean, because the boy will be a Nazirite of God from birth until the day of his death.'"*

It is reasonable to believe that Yahweh had chosen this family because they still held strong spiritual beliefs in how to worship their God. We see this in how Manoah responded to his wife. First, he went directly to prayer. He didn't try to correct his wife or to put her down. In fact, he was looking to have a similar experience. He wanted to meet with this angel so that he too could feel the same joy in his heart that his wife was now feeling.

Second, Manoah understood the seriousness of the message his wife had received. He knew that they were being given a huge responsibility. They would be in charge of raising a son who would begin to lead the entire nation of Israel out of their current bondage. Manoah not only wanted the angel to return to hear the news himself, but he wanted the angel to return so that they would be taught all they needed to know to teach their son the true message. They wanted to have supernatural Holy Spirit-led teachings that would put them on the right path to success. I wonder what we would be like if we got down on our knees and prayed this way regularly when raising our children or over our actions in our workplace.

Because of their sincerity and desire to be spirit led, God answered their requests. The angel of God again returned to the woman as she was sitting out in a field. It is interesting that this woman is not named, but God sees her as an extremely important person that should be lifted up to a higher level of respect. Twice the angel appeared to her without her husband being around. If the Lord could predict the future and know exactly what this child would become and do for their nation, I believe that the Lord would have known when to arrive at their camp to give them the news.

Manoah passes the next test of obedience to God as his wife sought him out and asks him to return with her to see the angel. The woman had again run to find him. She was eager to get this out in the open once and for all. She needed her husband to believe her. This was a way to remove all doubt that he might have had. You know those looks that men give when they say they believe you, but somewhere in the back of their minds they cannot really put it all together? Manoah's wife may have felt that look.

Manoah gets up and follows her to where the angel is waiting in the field. Either Manoah isn't all that bright or he truly didn't get it. It seems that everyone we read about in the scriptures seems to be aware that they are in the presence of a being that is not of this world. Something about them gives away their true status. Good grief, his wife was able to see an angel standing there!

So here is Manoah coming into the field and instead of asking the questions that he had asked God about how to teach, instead the first question he comes up with is, "Are you the man who spoke to this woman?" Well, two things we can pick up on: he can only see a man standing there; and second, he doesn't address his wife by any other title than "this woman".

The angel flatly answers, "Yes." Now Manoah begins to ask a few good questions about what his son's role should be in the scheme of things and what is he to do. You can just see Manoah trying to take over the situation here in this passage. Interestingly enough the angel repeats the instructions exactly as before. The woman is supposed to follow all of the directions that had been given to her. Here the angel does repeat the directions for Manoah's curiosity.

After being put into his place Manoah rises to the occasion by asking the angel to stay a little longer so that they may serve him some bread and meat from a kid. The Lord then said that he would not eat, but would accept a burnt offering. Still Manoah did not realize that this was actually the Lord God!

Manoah asks the man for his name. The Lord asks; "Why do you ask to know my name?" In other words, you are so dumb that you still don't get it. Okay, here is a new clue for you. My name is too wonderful for you to know! Manoah brings out the gift offering and sets it on a rock. This time he sets it down to him who works wonders.

The rock shoots up a flame toward heaven as it consumes the offering. The angel of God disappears into the flame directly in front of them. Finally, Manoah truly understands that he was in the presence of God. Then panic sets in and he believes that they are going to die since they met with God. Again his wife sets him straight, saying that God had accepted their offering and if they were to die what was the point in giving them the command to raise their son to be a nazirite.

They rested in the fact that they were blessed in this encounter. Their son Sampson was born, and as he grew the Lord continued to bless him. The spirit of the Lord began to grow within Sampson and he felt power in seeking his new direction.

A Word on the Philistines

Genesis 10:14 introduces the people group known as the Philistines. They are the descendants of Ham the son of Noah. This verse says that they come from Caphtorin.

Many scholars have tried to place the final location where this people group ended up. The longer list that the Philistines are part of includes: Cush, Egypt, Put, and Canaan. The region from Egypt up through Israel is called the Levant. It is in these regions that these tribes spread out to fill and to conquer.

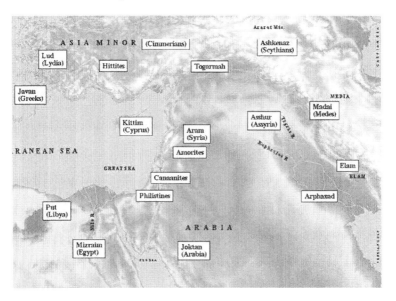

This map[17] is one representation of where the descents of Noah spread out to repopulate the earth. We can see from this map several of the previous enemies the Israelites have had to face. The Syrians, Amorites, and the

---

17

http://www.austingrad.edu/images/Resources/Shipp/Maps/TableofNations.jpg

Canaanites are from the north and Egyptians from the south.

Many scholars and students of the Bible simply cannot agree on the placement of the Philistines. The simplest placement would be as seen on this map because of the Philistine's physical location in the book of Judges. Some have believed that they were a people group that came from the sea. In other words, they sailed in and conquered the land just as the Vikings did in our era.

Robert Alexander Stewart Macalister published an extensive report in 1913 simply titled "The Philistines". This book can be found online at sacred-text.com. Macalister began his career with an interest in Irish archeology, but he developed a strong interest in biblical archeology. He and his colleague Frederick J. Bless excavated several towns in the Shephelah region which is part of Palestine. They performed these excavations in the years 1898 to 1900.

In chapter I of "The Philistines" Macalister gives an extensive lesson on the research used to find the true location of the Philistines. He started with the text in Genesis and the other texts found within scripture.[18] These gave him his first clues on where to look within the region. He was able to find significant leads in the Egyptian writing where there was much discussion of a people group

---

[18] Page 4

from the island of Crete that would invade Egypt different during time periods.[19] The name of the city, Caphtor, appears in writings on stone tablets both on the island of Crete and in Egypt. It is possible that this city name comes from their ancestor Caphtorin.

A Mother's Sad Tale of a Spoiled Son

I now understand the futility of telling moms of wayward children that it wasn't their fault. I truly meant it when I told them that I saw them doing all of the correct parenting things in raising their children. I was one of the "they" that had all of the answers. I meant well. What did I know when I didn't have one of my own to deal with. I now have come full cycle and I know in my heart that Sampson was raised right.

I had it good from the start. The angel of the Lord swooped into my life when I had all but given up hope on having my own child. I set my life apart during those years to live for a time as a Nazirite just as I was directed to do. I saw evidence in Sampson's life while he was growing up that he was so special in so many ways. He had talents that others didn't have. I also followed the directions that God gave me.

---

[19] Pages 9 - 15

Sampson has never had wine or other strong drink. I made sure to instruct him not to go near, or to play with, things that had died; and I never, ever cut his hair even though at times it would get so tangled up. Oy vey! There were days I could see the blessing of the Lord just drip off from him. I guess that is why I am now so disappointed in how his life turned out.

Well, I guess I should tell you why I am so upset with Sampson. It started back in his late youth when he was looking to take a bride. No matter how hard Manoah and I talked with him about finding the right girl to help him in his life's mission he kept going down into the valley to see those Philistine girls. Looking back on it now, I can understand his problem.

Those girls didn't behave the way our girls do. These girls had an allure to them. I think just because they are not part of our culture and of our heritage. They were elusive and tempting.

One day after taking a trip down to Timnah in the Sorek Valley he came back with the crazy idea of taking one of those girls for his wife. He marched right into our home and demanded that we get her for a bride. Together Manoah and I ran through an entire laundry list of reasons

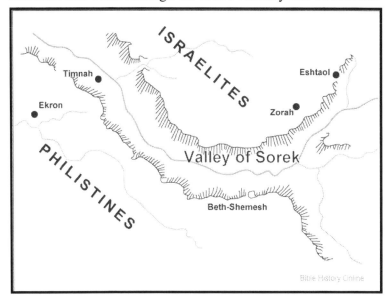

why this was wrong. We racked our brains trying to show him the options that were here in our area. In fact, we were willing to go to all the way to the northern reaches of Israel to Mardon to get him a bride.

He wouldn't hear of it. All he could think about was how she pleased him. What does a young man know about being pleased? It takes years for a couple to learn how to be fully pleased with each other. I tried to tell him that beauty fades with time; one must look for other important aspects to find true pleasure. Like I said, he wouldn't hear of it. What I didn't know at the time is that God would use his problems with the Philistines to begin the process of getting rid of those people from our country.

Sampson got Manoah and me to go down to Timnah to meet the family of this girl. Somehow, on the way, we got separated. We must not walk as fast as we once did. I found out later that Sampson was walking by some grape vines when a young lion roared at him. He said that suddenly he felt a rush of power surge through him that could only have come from God. Well, that lion paid dearly for venturing so close to where people lived. My Sampson literally tore him apart with his bare hands. I am sure that he didn't tell us because this would have been against his Nazirite code.

While we were there it became obvious to us that no matter how much talking we would do we would lose. So, since she pleased him so much, we made plans for the wedding. Weddings for us are a big deal with much planning involved. A wedding is not just a one day event; no, we allow for seven days of merriment full of drinking and much laughter. However, *our* wedding feast was not at all a happy one.

More on that subject later. First, I need to finish the story of the lion. On the way to the wedding festival Sampson had noticed the lion's body had some bees swarming around it. His curiosity got the best of him and he went ahead to explore. Manoah and I must have been deep into one of our conversations, if you know what I mean, and didn't see what Sampson was doing.

Sampson saw that the bees had been making honey inside of the carcass. He scooped out the honey and brought it to us without telling us again where it had come from. This is the second time that he defiled himself with something dead. I guess silence is better than getting a lecture from your mother.

We went on to see the woman he was going to marry and Sampson went to have a feast with the young men of Timnah. The people of the town saw him and made sure that thirty of their young men came to be with him for companionship. After all, he was from out of town; how would he know who to feast with? This was nice of them.

Sampson began to put on some of his airs, you know, a haughty, arrogant little attitude. When the young men arrived he offered them a riddle to figure out. With this riddle he further offered the challenge to complete it within the seven days of their feast. If one of them was able to figure the riddle out he would give them thirty linen garments and an additional festal garment. He then went on to say that if they couldn't find the answer then they would have to give the equivalent to him. I heard that they all agreed to the terms.

His riddle went like this:

"Out of the eater came something to eat,
out of the strong came something sweet."

The festival went on for three days with the young men being unable to complete the task of answering the riddle. Finally, they gave up doing it on their own and they certainly didn't want to lose to an Israelite. I heard that those young men took Sampson's wife aside and threatened to burn her and her father's house with fire if she didn't get the answer to the riddle from her husband. She had put both her family and her culture at stake. Those young men accused her of bringing them down low and causing them to lose their money.

Here we, Manoah and I, are in the middle of our son's wedding feast; which, in my memory, have always been happy, joyous occasions. Apparently it was not a joyous occasion for Sampson's wife; she came at him with such a force of words! Those young men were acting like little boys who were afraid of getting the wrong answer in class.

They instilled such fear in her that she went to Sampson and she literally broke down weeping before him. She was demanding that he give to her an answer to his riddle. You could hear her accusing my son of not really loving her, in fact she blamed him for hating her. She began to pout because he had not fully explained the riddle to her.

Sampson, confused by all of this attention, claimed that he didn't even tell his father or me the riddle. This is true. We would have told him not to get high in his saddle and try to be better than them, so as not to cause more trouble than necessary.

Each day the festival went on became the same as the last for those two, Sampson and his wife. He tried to make light of the situation and she just kept coming at him with those eyes red from crying nonstop. Finally, on the last day she came at him with everything she had. I told Manoah that she was the biggest nag I had ever known. My poor Sampson tried to make peace with her and her family so he finally broke down and told her the whole truth behind the riddle.

She went off grateful that her family would not suffer from this event. I am sorry that she had to choose between the two, especially with what happens next. The men came to Sampson just before sunset and gave him their answer to the riddle. Their answer was:

"What is sweeter than honey?
What is stronger than a lion?"[20]

Sampson may not be the brightest young man, but he was able to know where their answer came from. He accused them directly, in front of us all, of messing with his wife. Sampson was good to his word and went out to get

---

[20] NRVS Judges 14:18b

the clothes that he had promised. This is where I can now see the Lord began the work in fighting against the Israelites.

My son became filled with the Lord's spirit. In fact, I know that this spirit rushed over him and gave to him extra-ordinary strength, power and courage. He went out from the party and traveled over thirty miles to the coastal town of Ashkelon. It was in this Philistine town that Sampson killed thirty men and took from them the spoils needed to pay off his debt back in Timnah.

Sampson's Righteous Revenge

Sampson was done with his wife and with the people of Timnah so he returned home with us. We had heard that Sampson's wife's father gave her over to Sampson's best man at the wedding. Sampson stewed over this for a long time. He waited until it was harvest time in the valley and went back to see his wife.

Sampson had brought with him a gift for the family. He wanted to give them a young goat. I know in Sampson's mind he had not abandoned his wife as others had assumed. My son thought that he could go to her anytime that he desired. I know that this comes from our tradition of being married for life. Sampson tried to get to her room, but her father stood up to him and refused his entry. He did; though, offer Sampson another daughter that was prettier. Sampson would not hear of it and again became embroiled in his anger.

He called out to him; "If you think I did wrong to your people last time, so be it, this time I have a reason for what is to come." So there was Sampson in the middle of their fields looking to come up with a plan. There it came to him a great plan of revenge.

Sampson went out into the fields and the hedgerows and caught three hundred foxes. He tied their tails together in pairs. He also weaved a torch into each one of those pairs. Sampson made sure that he had enough foxes for all of the fields that were dry and ready for harvest. He also went to the vineyard and to the groves of olive trees. Sampson went as fast as he could go, setting fire to the torches, and then setting the foxes loose to create a raging fire.

When the Philistines found out who had created such a disaster in their livelihood, they set out for their own revenge. They discovered that Sampson was the son-in-law of the Timnite and that he had given Sampson's wife away. That little girl had tried to save her family and her community, but in the end it was all destroyed. The Philistines came into town and burned her and her father up.

My son was again filled with rage that they would take out their frustration on his wife and father-in-law.

Sampson met their outrage with some of his own. Now he was without his wife and he vowed to take out his full revenge on all of the Philistines. He began to slaughter all of those who were part of his personal loss. When he was finished he went to hide in the rocks by Etam, just south of Bethlehem.

Revenge is Never Finished

I wish I could tell you that this story of revenge had ended with this one battle. It didn't. The Philistines who survived went for help and they were able to track my Sampson down in the rocky area in the hills of Judah. It was there the Philistines made an encampment and raided Lehi.

The men of Judah confronted the Philistines and asked them what they had done to cause this attack on them. After hearing the news, the men from Judah took about three thousand of their bravest to bring Sampson back to face the Philistines.

The men of Judah found Sampson hiding in Etam. It was there that they confronted him with his out-of-control behavior against the Philistines. These warriors wanted to know if my Sampson was confused about who was truly the ruler of this land. More important to their thinking, they asked Sampson why he would upset the natural order of things. They asked him if he knew that his actions had put the whole nation at risk.

Lest you forget the reason for my son, let me remind you that together, we as a nation, had forgotten our allegiance to our God, Yahweh. We have been under the control of the Philistines because of our sinful desires that turned us away from Yahweh. Because of this, Yahweh had, and continues to, give us over to these uncircumcised people. What these men from Judah didn't know, but I do because the Lord met with me so many years ago, is that my son Sampson will begin to bring these people down.

I should finish this part of the story and not get to preaching. Sampson had the warriors agree not to kill him, but to take him back to where the Philistines were encamped. He also allowed them to bind him tight with ropes. These brave warriors witnessed a huge slaughter when they arrived back at the Philistine camp.

The Philistines, when they saw Sampson, couldn't control themselves and came running up to him shouting their curses. Again the power of the Lord flowed through Sampson's veins. He broke those ropes as easily as fire rips through dry stalks of flax. Let me put it a different way. The rope literally melted off his arms like hot butter.

Lying on the ground nearby, Sampson noticed a donkey jawbone. He took this bone that had dried meat and flesh still on it and began to swing it about as those

Philistines kept charging at him. The men of Judah just looked on as a thousand men died that day. Sampson turned to those three thousand men and said to them:

"With the jawbone of a donkey, heaps upon heaps, with the jawbone of a donkey I have slain a thousand men."

Sampson was tired and thirsty after this battle and asked the Lord God to be refreshed. The Lord split a rock open and fresh cool water came springing out. After Sampson drank from this he was totally refreshed.

Those men went back to their homes telling others what had happened on that hill. Later as the story was retold over and over again the place took the name, "The Hill of the Jawbone". The story of Sampson raced around the entire region and then began to spread to the entire nation. From that point on, my son Sampson was the judge over Israel. He was the judge for twenty years.

One Last Sad Story to Tell

I want you to know that I am truly proud of my son and all that he accomplished for Israel. It is just that he had problems controlling his thought life and his actions when it came to the opposite sex. He just couldn't stay away from the allure of those Philistine women. Like the time that he went all the way down to the coastal city of Gaza to find a prostitute.

He went down to spend the night with her. The people of Gaza realized who had come into their town. Quietly they circled around the house and waited all night. Many went to the gate to make sure that it was locked, so that if he got past the others, he would still be trapped.

I am sure that the spirit of the Lord was again with my boy. He finished with the prostitute around midnight and decided to head on home. The men of the city had hoped to kill him in the morning when the light was breaking over the mountains. Instead, Sampson was able to sneak past the guards. When he saw the gates closed my boy simply pulled the door and the post up out of the[21] ground. Just to make a point he carried the gates across the plain and up onto the mountain. He didn't stop until he reached the town of Hebron some forty miles away. I'm sure that the men of Hebron wanted to have another city gate.

Now Sampson fell in love again. He was finally over the pain of the passing of his first wife. Delilah was also from the valley of Sorek. The leaders of the Philistines kept track of Sampson and soon realized that he had fallen in love with Delilah. They quietly kept coming to her to see if she could find out what made my son, Sampson, so strong. Finally, she agreed to the plan when they offered here eleven hundred pieces of silver. Now, I don't know

---

[21] UNKNOWN; Illustrator of 'L'Histoire du Vieux et du Nouveau Testament', Nicolas Fontaine (author), 1670

about you, but that is a lot of money. In my day that would have caused almost anyone to trade in a lover. It helped her to erase the memory of what happened to his first wife and father-in-law.

So it was that Delilah began to ask Sampson what made him strong. Sampson's arrogance was growing too strong for him. He thought that he could get out of anything by now. So he played along with her games. First, he said that if he was bound by seven fresh bowstrings he would be weak. That night as he slept she tried it, but when she woke him in the middle of the night to tell him the Philistines were attacking he snapped them off, just as they did on The Hill of the Jawbone.

Delilah was not deterred from her task. This time when asked Sampson said that fresh ropes would bind him. The same thing happened that night. He threw the ropes off and mocked them in their attempts. Delilah though was extremely upset and told him that she was embarrassed and couldn't stand that he was lying to her.

Delilah simply would not be put off. The thought of that silver was more precious than Sampson's love for her. So on another occasion she asked Sampson again what caused him to become weak. Now, he really was toying with her by saying that if his hair was weaved into seven locks that were bound together he would be weak. Like I said, my son is not the brightest. That night Delilah played with his hair and again she called in the men of the town and again tried to catch him at a weak moment. They lost and they were beginning to lose patience with Delilah as well.

This time Delilah picked up where his first wife left off. She continued to nag him until he couldn't stand it any longer. He told her the full truth about being a Nazirite and the rules that go along with it. He said that he couldn't drink wine or touch things that had died. The last was the only rule that he hadn't broken so far and that was allowing a razor to cut his hair.

That night as Sampson slept; Delilah cut my son's hair. This time when the men of the valley came rushing in upon my Sampson he had no strength to hold them back. I am saddened to say that they took my son and tore out his eyes. They then put him into bronze shackles and led him away to Gaza. There he was on public display as he went around in circles pushing the stakes coming out of the millstone. Daily he was humiliated by those who once ran in fear of him. Not only was Sampson on display, but so was what he represented. They laughed at his God as well.

Conclusion

With my final time with you I want to let you know that in the end Sampson got his final revenge. The Philistines were holding a large party and they were worshiping their god Dagon. Someone had the idea to bring in Sampson as proof that Dagon was all-powerful. They wanted Sampson to perform for them as they delighted in how great they were and how great Dagon was.

What they didn't consider is that over time Sampson's hair had begun to grow back. Sampson found himself placed between two pillars that supported the entire roof. The Philistines were lost in their merriment as they watched Sampson perform. Sampson, in middle of the noise and entertainment, called out to God for the opportunity to revenge those who did this to him. I am sure that he also made his peace with Yahweh as well.

Sampson could feel the power of the Lord's spirit come over his muscles again. He called out over the din so that all could hear: "Let me die with the Philistines."[22] That day over three thousand leaders of the Philistines died with my son. I am told that he killed more in that one moment than he did in his whole life.

His brothers and I carried him home to be with his father who was buried there between the towns of Zorah and Eshtaol. My son judged Israel for twenty years.

Let me end with this; our sin caused us to be servants of these Philistines. It was our sin that kept us from coming back. We never knew that those things that

---

[22] NRSV Judges 16:30

lured us away would keep us away for so long. I am glad that I serve a God who is faithful to me even though I have wandered so far away. God keeps finding new ways to bring me back and continues to call me even when I don't want to hear. Will you learn from our lessons and our weakness? Don't be trapped like us. Sin is a terrible master in the end. It causes so much damage to all that it comes into contact with.

I want you to know that God even used my son who led his life through his lustful desires. He was used to begin the process of bringing down the Philistines.

May the Lord of all give you the gift of the Holy Spirit to give you the power that my son Sampson had. Amen

Monday

Secrets Prevent Growth

Sampson knew that touching the lion after it was dead was a breach to his nazirite code of conduct. When he examined the body and found the honey, he could have walked away, or he could have had his father come and help him retrieve the honey. Instead, he took the honey and offered it as a gift to his parents who at the time still had some authority over his life.

What about our lives and our commitment to God's call on our life? Through the calling of the Holy Spirit we have recognized our relationship with the Triune God. As our love deepens for God, so our desire to please God grows deeper and fuller. Even in the midst of this growth we find times that we are tempted to act out to fulfill our personal desires to give a gift to ourselves. Our rationale, just like Sampson's, is that it is only honey. What harm can it cause to taste just some of it?

Sampson must have known that he was not acting in a right manner since he withheld key information from his parents. In fact, he lured them into his sin as well by offering them a gift obtained in a sinful fashion.

What "good thing" is luring you away from the center of God's love? You may know because you are trying to keep it a secret or trying to give it away to others.

TUESDAY

SIN BLINDS

Sampson enters into a relationship with his first wife and also with Delilah where he is blinded by his desires for them. He desires to please them and forgets his mission to remove the Philistines from the Israelite land. These two women have control over his actions. Sure, Sampson resisted at first, but this was out of his arrogance. These two women beat him down to the point that he gives in to their repeated requests.

Is there something beating you down today that will lead you to a sinful action?

When Sampson was tricked by his wife and by the young men of the town he avoided the real issue of his guilt in the murder of thirty men by blaming others for his misdeed. When we give in to our sinful desires, don't we do the same and blame others for our actions?

Reflect on this and see where God is leading you.

WEDNESDAY

POINT TO CONSIDER

Scripture reveals that God is consistent. This is important for us on many different levels. We know that we can trust the word of God since it is not filled with situational ethics. We can stand firm in knowing that what God said four thousand years ago still stands today. We don't have to worry that the rules will change from day to day.

One example where God has remained consistent is that the Bible speaks of only three persons who lived their entire life as a nazirite. They are Sampson, Samuel and John the Baptist. Each of these men had three things in common: their mothers had been barren; they had a special appointment with God's messenger; they were told that their child was set apart to accomplish a specific mission that would bring praise and glory to God.

What are some consistencies that God has shown in dealing with your life?

Does this give you confidence that God will be consistent with you tomorrow?

THURSDAY

GOD'S GRACE

Sampson had been guilty of being arrogant and playing too close with his sinful desires. As a result, he lost his freedom to Delilah and her companions. He was led off to Gaza blinded and in bronze shackles. It was there that he was put on public display. He was being used in an attempt to show that Baal Dagon was stronger than Yahweh.

Sampson was brought out to perform at a special event in front of all the great Philistine leaders. Sampson, at the end of his human strength, finally submitted himself to God and the mission that had been given to him.

When Sampson was in place to do the most damage to his enemies he asked God for one last chance to fulfill his destiny. God's spirit again flowed through his body. God gave Sampson the strength and courage needed to complete the task. God had given a once arrogant, selfish Sampson grace, or in our modern thought process, forgiveness.

Do you practice on a regular basis opening your heart to God and allowing God to offer you forgiveness for all those times in your life where you have fallen short of doing it right? If not, today is a good time to begin.

Friday

God Works in the Mysterious

In the end, our desire was not to show you, the reader, how great Deborah, Gideon, or Sampson were, but instead to introduce you to a living God who is truly the main character.

God uses the natural world to fight battles for us.

God uses the weak to accomplish great things.

God even uses sinful people to bring about the desired results for the people of God.

It is our responsibility to look for God in all of these places so that we don't miss out on the blessing that God has for us.

Know today that God is with us, for us and working in us to bring Glory to the Trinity.

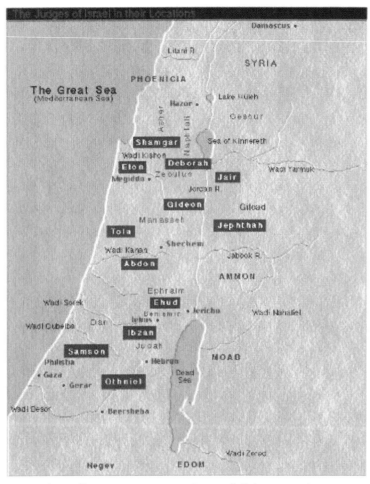

http://www.preceptaustin.org/bible_maps.htm

STEPHEN CROWELL

For most of Stephen's childhood he lived on what was his grandparent's farm in Western New York. The forests were his playground. At the time he loved the winter months, building ice forts and skiing on the back hill. Now; though, Stephen has a hard time with the winter's cold and snow after living all over the southern states of America.

Stephen was fortunate to have served as youth and young adult pastor under his father in two different Wesleyan Churches. He then was asked to serve a small rural church in Leon, New York which is famous for their Amish community. While serving as a pastor, Stephen completed his Outdoor-Recreation degree from Houghton College. This degree came in handy when Stephen served as a camp director for the United Methodist Church in Pennsylvania.

Currently Stephen is serving as a senior pastor back in Western New York for the United Methodist Church. His passion has been working to develop an emerging church model. Stephen desires to bring people back to the radical message that Jesus taught his disciples. We have a responsibility to be in close intimate fellowship groups that help to support each other through the good and the bad.

Jesus also taught us to have an outward looking focus. Stephen understands that the message of the cross is for those who are marginalized and are sitting on the fringes. He believes that we need to break down all barriers to the foot of the cross. Another area that Stephen feels is important for the community of Christ's followers is to come together regularly to share common meals. It seems that scripture is regularly depicting Jesus eating with friends, relatives, strangers, and most importantly sinners.

Stephen is dedicated to spending any and all spare time traveling with his wife, Kristan, and with any of the kids that desire to come along. They have eight children, one of which is a daughter-in-law. They now use the excuse that the kids live in different parts of the country to visit with them. (Texas, Alaska, Florida)

If this book has helped you with your life's journey Stephen would love to hear from you. If you have a story about how this book has helped you, or changed your life, please share it with him @ pastor@konxions.org.

May God bless you on your journey.
Pastor Stephen Crowell

L. E. Capodagli

I must confess right off the bat that I am not one who has ever sought to master that esoteric art of writing about myself in the third person. As a result, this may end up sounding like a cross between a "personal" ad and an adult's version of that old fourth-grade assignment "What I did last summer." So be it; to quote that great spinach-lovin' hunk of a man: "I yam what I yam."

I was raised by my Mom, and, bless her soul, a succession of beautiful dogs. Mom was widowed early in her marriage to Dad and never remarried. I grew up an only child without neighbors in beautiful country. There were creeks and a lake to play and fish in, beaver ponds to run a trap line, meadows and woods in which to build my forts and tree houses and a universe full of room in which to just imagine that anything could be.

For the vast majority of my life I have lived in that beautiful country, in my ancestral family home down on the old Creek Road in Western New York, in a small hamlet that doesn't really exist anymore except in a series of old stone-walled cellar foundations scattered up and down both sides of a couple miles of country road. McGrawville--a small but thriving country community--disappeared sometime in the late 1800's; no one knows why. Oh, it's on a lot of old maps, it had a post office, churches, a newspaper; the early land baron of Allegany County had his famous horse racing stable there; and then--gone. I guess you wouldn't be too far off base to say I grew up in a ghost town. Perhaps that's why some people describe me as having a "scary" personality. (Just a little personal humor there to make you more comfortable; people don't really say that about me—well, not *all* of them.)

Now, I'm going be rather hard pressed to tell you when I first met Christ. To me, that's kind of like asking me when I first realized I was a person; I just always have been. With apologies (I guess) to those who have asked me, "How can you know you have an end in Christ if you never had a beginning in Him?" all I can say is just that I have always known there was a God. It was just natural. You may as well have felt it necessary to tell me the sky was blue: like this is something that I am supposed to *not* know?

This knowledge, however, had never had such a direct impact on my life as it has in the last two and a half years. After a short stint of being provided with free room and board courtesy of the State Of New York, I emerged from that experience with a new view on my life--a life that I had almost lost lying in an ICU a few months earlier. I decided, right then and there, to consciously, deliberately and specifically live for Christ in a manner that I realized I had been studiously avoiding for many years.

During these past thirty months I have moved three times, had to give up my dogs (the apartment thing) joined this, been elected to that: and met Stephen and his family.

My debt to them for their kindness, friendship, encouragement, gentle (and sometimes not-so-gentle) prodding, the opportunity to work and write with Stephen, has become, and will remain, immeasurable. They gave me a chance; and that's all I was asking. Thank you, guys--muchly.

If you are wondering what I did in those long years when I lived with Christ on my tongue but not in my heart: I mowed roughs at a golf course, worked as a short-order cook in a greasy spoon, served as Assistant Manager in a group home for psychiatric patients and worked as a clothier printer; piled boards in a lumber yard, did some construction demolition, served as Assistant Cook in a four star restaurant--and dug graves. (Grave digging is good work; it's quiet, peaceful, contemplative, lonely work--I like that.) I know there are a few--or more than a few--other no-account jobs in there that I just don't remember, but that's about it: jack-of-all trades, master of none.

If you have any questions, comments or criticisms relating to this book--or anything, actually-I'm not shy--don't hesitate to yip me up at leecap@konxions.org. I'm always glad to meet new people. And if you happen to hear of a reasonable apartment, a good-looking hunting dog puppy, or a fine Christian woman who is available, please let me know; I'm looking for all three.

Thank you, bless you, and may God be with you.
Lee Capodagli

Made in the USA
Charleston, SC
29 December 2011